LEVEL

3

Fact Reader

Sharks!

100 FUN Facts About These Fin-tastic Fish

Stephanie Warren Drimmer

NATIONAL GEOGRAPHIC

Washington, D.C.

For Sloane, my little fish —S.W.D.

Published by National Geographic Partners, LLC,
Washington, D.C. 20036.

Designed by Gus Tello

Author's Note
The author and publisher gratefully acknowledge
the expert content review of this book by
Christopher G. Lowe, Ph.D., professor of marine
biology and director of the Shark Lab, California
State University, Long Beach, and the literacy review
by Mariam Jean Dreher, professor emerita of read-
ing education, University of Maryland, College Park.

Photo Credits
AL = Alamy Stock Photo; BP = Blue Planet
Archive; AS = Adobe Stock; GI = Getty Images;
NGIC = National Geographic Image Collection;
NGP = National Geographic Partners, LLC;
NP = Nature Picture Library; SS = Shutterstock
Cover (CTR), Reinhard Dirscherl/GI; 1 (CTR), frantisek
hojdysz/AS; 3 (LE), Ryan M. Bolton/SS; 3 (CTR), Bert
Folsom/AL; 3 (RT), Ryan M. Bolton/SS; 4 (UP LE),
Andy Murch/NP; 4 (UP RT), warpaintcobra/AS; 4
(CTR LE), www.pqpictures.co.uk/AL; 4 (LO), wildest-
animal/AS; 5 (UP RT), David Shen/BP; 5 (UP LE),
BillionPhotos.com/AS; 5 (CTR LE), BlueSnap/SS; 5
(CTR RT), izenkai/AS; 5 (LO LE), Shawn/AS; 5 (LO RT),
JoLin/SS; 6-7, Rodrigo Friscione/AL; 7 (UP LE), Saul
Gonor/BP; 7 (UP RT), Andrey Armyagov/AS; 8,
Franco Tempesta/NGP; 8 (LO), ribeiroantonio/SS; 9,
SS/SS; 9 (LO), scubagreg123/AS; 10, tank200bar/SS;
11 (LO), Ian Scott/SS; 11 (UP), by wildestanimal/GI; 12,
David Doubilet/NGIC; 13 (LO LE), Ryan/AS; 13 (LO RT),
the Ocean Agency/AS; 14, Patrick_Gijsbers/GI; 15,
Doug Perrine/NP; 16-17, Mike Workman/SS; 16 (LO),
Alex Hyde/NP; 18 (LO), David Gruber/NGIC; 18 (UP),
Mark Conlin/BP; 19, Espen Rekdal/BP; 20, Alastair
Pollock Photography/GI; 21, Andrea Izzotti/AL; 22,
Andy Murch/BP; 23 (UP), Greg Lecoeur/NGIC; 23
(LO), LITTLE DINOSAUR/GI; 24, Uryadnikov Sergey/
AS; 25 (UP), Norbert Probst/GI; 25 (LO), NiCK/GI; 26
(UP), wildestanimal/AS; 26 (LO), Auscape/UIG/SS;
27 (UP), Gregory Sweeney/GI; 27 (LO), ArteSub/AL;
28, Jan Finsterbusch/SS; 28 (LO LE), Alex
Mustard/2020VISION/NP; 29 (LO), Stephen Kajiura;
30, Chris & Monique Fallows/NP; 31 (UP), Franco
Tempesta/NGP; 31 (LO), Bill Curtsinger/NGIC; 32,
Brian J. Skerry/NGIC; 33 (UP), Kelvin Aitken/VWPics/
AL; 33 (CTR), Nick Caloyianis/NGIC; 33 (LO), John
Morrissey/BP; 34 (LO LE), wildestanimal/SS; 34
(CTR RT), Michael Patrick O'Neill/BP; 35 (UP), Kelvin
Aitken/V&W/Image Quest Marine; 35 (LO), Bruce
Rasner/Jeffrey Rotman/Biosphoto; 35 (UP RT), Kelvin
Aitken/V&W/Image Quest Marine; 36, Franco
Tempesta/NGP; 37 (UP), Franco Tempesta/NGP;
37 (LO LE), Franco Tempesta/NGP; 38-39, Willem
Kolvoort/NP; 39 (UP RT), Norbert Wu/Minden
Pictures; 40, wildestanimal/GI; 41 (UP RT), Daniel/
AS; 41 (CTR LE), Media Drum World/AL; 41 (LO RT),
Michael Flippo/AS; 42-43, Andy Murch/BP; 43 (LO
RT), Martin Strmiska/BP; 44 (teeth), Mark Kostich/AS;
44-45 (LO CTR), Aaron/AS; 44 (UP LE), Masa
Ushioda/BP; 44 (CTR LE), Brian J. Skerry/NGIC; 44
(RT), Stephen Frink/GI; 45 (UP LE), Derek Heasley/SS;
45 (UP RT), Tomas Kotouc/SS; 45 (CTR RT), Michael
Aw/NGIC; 45 (CTR LE), Unique Vision/AS; 45 (CTR
RT), grafffik/AS

**Library of Congress Cataloging-in-Publication
Data**

Names: Drimmer, Stephanie Warren, author.
Title: Sharks! : 100 fun facts about these fin-tastic
    fish / Stephanie Warren Drimmer.
Description: Washington, D.C. : National
    Geographic Kids, 2022. | Series: National
    geographic readers | Audience: Ages 7-9 |
    Audience: Grades 2-3
Identifiers: LCCN 2021049832 (print) | LCCN
    2021049833 (ebook) | ISBN 9781426372704
    (paperback) | ISBN 9781426373626 (library
    binding) | ISBN 9781426374425 (ebook other) |
    ISBN 9781426374432 (ebook)
Subjects: LCSH: Sharks--Juvenile literature.
Classification: LCC QL638.9 .D75 2022 (print) | LCC
    QL638.9 (ebook) | DDC 597.3--dc23/
    eng/20211014
LC record available at https://lccn.loc
    .gov/2021049832
LC ebook record available at https://lccn.loc
    .gov/2021049833

Printed in the United States of America
22/WOR/1

Contents

1 Lantern sharks glow in the dark.

2 In 2005, scientists tracked a great white shark as it traveled 12,400 miles from Africa to Australia.

3 Adult female sharks are almost always bigger than adult male sharks.

4 Almost everything scientists know about shark evolution comes from shark teeth—usually the only thing left behind by prehistoric sharks.

5 Prehistoric megalodon was the largest shark that ever lived. It was 60 feet long—that's almost as long as a bowling lane!

6 Shark skin feels rough, like sandpaper.

7 It may not look like it, but sharks have ears—they're just inside their heads.

8 Sharks can only swim forward.

9 A great white shark can eat up to 11 tons of food in a year. That's about 11 times more than the average human eats!

10 Great white sharks are named for their white bellies.

25 COOL FACTS ABOUT SHARKS

11
Some sharks will enter a trancelike state when they are flipped onto their backs.

12
A few shark species live in freshwater rivers in India, Southeast Asia, and parts of Australia.

13
The goblin shark looks almost the same as it did 125 million years ago, when dinosaurs roamed Earth.

14
To figure out how old a shark is, scientists can look at a piece of its spine and count the bands like the rings of a tree.

15
Like cats, sharks have a reflective layer in their eyes that allows them to see well in the dark.

16
Basking sharks have been spotted traveling together in schools of 100.

17
Shortfin mako sharks can be 12 feet long and weigh 1,200 pounds.

18
Scientists believe that the Greenland shark may live for more than 400 years.

19
Walking sharks use their fins to "walk" along the seafloor—and sometimes even onto land!

20
The angel shark can attack and kill its prey in one-tenth of a second.

21
For most sharks, one-third of their brain is dedicated to their sense of smell.

22
Scientists think sharks may not see in color.

23
Great white sharks are the world's largest predatory fish, or fish that hunt.

24
Sixgill sharks can have more than 100 babies at a time.

25
A baby shark can sense a predator from inside its egg.
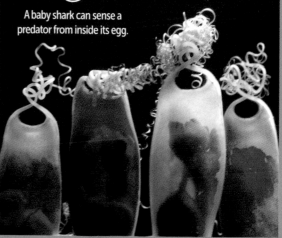

CHAPTER 1

Remarkable Sharks

Sharks have LARGE BRAINS for their body size and are capable of learning.

Sharks don't chew their food. THEY RIP OFF CHUNKS AND SWALLOW THEM WHOLE!

They swim in every ocean. They can be as small as a human's hand or as long as a city bus.

Sharks live in nearly **ALL OCEAN HABITATS,** from tropical reefs to chilly Arctic waters.

Greenland shark

Sharks are FISH.

blacktip reef shark

lemon shark

They can have bright pink skin, heads shaped like hammers, or mouths that open wider than their bodies. They're sharks, and they're some of the coolest creatures on Earth!

Ancient sharks once shared the seas with GIANT SWIMMING REPTILES called mosasaurs (MOH-zuh-sores) and plesiosaurs (PLEE-see-uh-sores).

an ancient shark

Sharks have been on Earth since BEFORE THE TIME OF THE DINOSAURS.

Sharks first appeared about 400 million years ago. Prehistoric sharks looked a lot like two modern species: frilled sharks and cow sharks. These species are sometimes called living fossils because they look just like the sharks from millions of years ago.

Scientists have found fossils of more than 3,000 SPECIES of PREHISTORIC SHARKS.

modern frilled shark

modern cow shark

9

Once they reach their adult size, SHARKS KEEP GROWING slowly for the rest of their lives.

grey reef shark

Sharks have no bones. Instead, their skeletons are made of cartilage (KART-uh-lij), the same bendy material that forms your ears and the tip of your nose. It's very strong, yet light and flexible. This helps sharks stay afloat and make tight turns as they swim.

Sharks use gills to breathe. These organs are behind the slits on the sides of their heads. As water passes over the gills, they take in oxygen. Some sharks have to keep swimming in order to breathe. Others can pump water over their gills so they can breathe even while resting on the ocean floor.

gill slits

sand tiger shark

spotted eagle ray

Sharks belong to a group of animals called ELASMOBRANCHS (ee-LAZ-muh-brangks), which also includes rays and skates.

11

A great white shark can grow 50,000 TEETH in its lifetime.

Sharks have mouths lined with many rows of teeth. When a tooth falls out, the one behind it moves forward to take its place. Sharks are always growing new teeth.

Shark teeth can be many different shapes. Some are like needles. They are good at holding on to slippery prey, such as squid. Others are jagged like a saw. They are good at cutting up larger prey. Still others are flat like plates. These are good at crushing prey with hard shells, such as shrimp or crabs.

shortfin mako shark

Some sharks replace their teeth EVERY TWO WEEKS.

bull shark

The outer coating of shark teeth is made of **FLUORIDE** (FLOOR-ide), the active ingredient in **TOOTHPASTE.**

Some sharks lay eggs that are protected by a tough, leathery pouch called an egg case. It is nicknamed a "mermaid's purse." Other sharks carry their eggs inside their bodies. The pups grow inside the eggs until they hatch and are born.

Baby sharks are called PUPS.

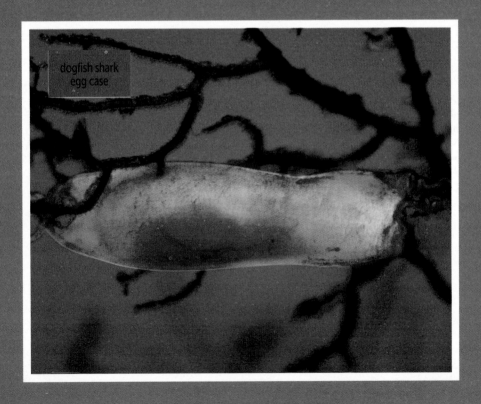

dogfish shark egg case

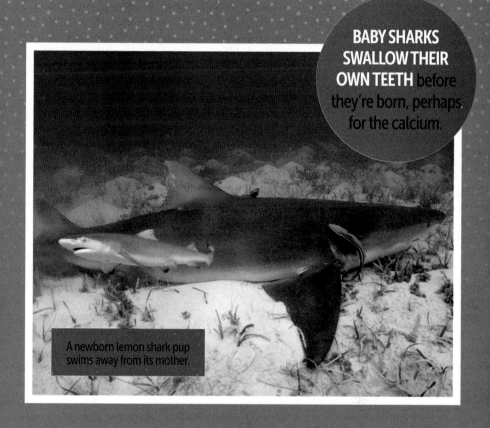

A newborn lemon shark pup swims away from its mother.

Still other sharks give birth to live young like humans do. The mother's body feeds the pups as they grow. But unlike human babies, shark pups have to fend for themselves from the moment they're born.

Before it's born, a sand tiger shark pup FEEDS ON its unborn SIBLINGS.

CHAPTER 2

Creature Features

A shark's skin can SHRED A DIVER'S WET SUIT.

Shark skin is made of millions of tiny V-shaped plates. Called denticles, they are more like teeth than fish scales. They are very sharp.

Denticles are about as HARD AS GRANITE and can ACT LIKE ARMOR.

whitetip reef shark

BY MIMICKING SHARK SKIN, designers are working to create **FASTER** airplanes, cars, and drones.

Tiny grooves in the denticles help water flow smoothly around a shark's body. This allows it to swim quickly and quietly, making it a sneaky hunter.

That's just one of the many features that make sharks some of the most amazing animals in the sea.

There are at least 57 SPECIES of sharks that CAN GLOW.

The SWELL SHARK scares off predators by gulping water and swelling to TWICE ITS NORMAL SIZE.

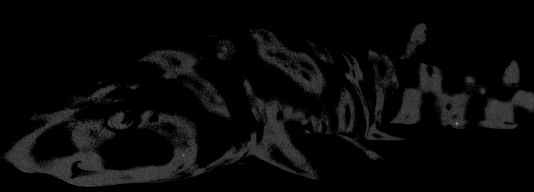

Humans have to use special tools to see a swell shark's green glow.

Scientists recently learned that swell sharks can create their own glow. The sharks have a special chemical in their skin. The chemical absorbs the blue light of the deep ocean and turns it into a bright green glow. Only other sharks can see this. Experts think the sharks may use this ability to communicate with each other.

The pocket shark can SQUIRT A GLOWING LIQUID, probably to distract predators.

velvet belly lantern shark

Sense-ational

Great white sharks can detect as little as ONE DROP OF BLOOD in 25 gallons of water.

Sharks are sometimes called swimming noses because of their strong sense of smell. But their other senses are impressive, too.

Sharks' eyes are adapted to see well underwater, where the light is often dim. They are especially good at spotting moving prey. Sharks can also hear prey from 3,000 feet away—that's a distance of more than eight football fields! They can even hear sounds that human ears can't detect, such as those made by a fish as it swims.

Sharks have taste buds lining their mouths and throats, and will SPIT OUT A MEAL they don't like.

Some sharks have SENSITIVE WHISKERS around their mouths that they use to TASTE THE OCEAN FLOOR, searching for buried prey.

nurse shark

spiny dogfish

Sharks have a sense organ called the lateral line. It is inside a shark's body and runs along both sides, under the skin. It can feel vibrations in the water and detect which way prey is moving and how fast it's going.

Sharks also have an extra sense called electro-reception. All living things give off electricity. Humans can't detect these faint electrical currents, but sharks can. They use special organs in their heads. Electroreception allows sharks to find prey hiding under sand on the seafloor.

electroreception pores

Great white sharks use electroreception to SENSE A FISH'S BREATHING.

blacktip reef shark

Using electroreception to sense Earth's magnetic field, sharks can swim in A PERFECTLY STRAIGHT LINE FOR MILES.

On the Hunt

Sharks are some of the most crafty predators on the planet. And each species uses different tricks to get a meal.

Researchers use DECOY SEALS to study great white sharks' hunting habits.

SNEAK ATTACK: Great white sharks often shoot up from below to catch prey, like seals, at the water's surface. They move so fast—around 25 miles an hour—that they can launch themselves out of the water.

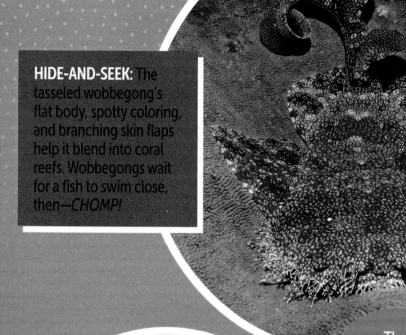

HIDE-AND-SEEK: The tasseled wobbegong's flat body, spotty coloring, and branching skin flaps help it blend into coral reefs. Wobbegongs wait for a fish to swim close, then—*CHOMP!*

The wobbegong's HUGE HEAD is wider than it is long.

SLAP HAPPY: A thresher shark's tail can be as long as its body. It uses its tail as a weapon, whipping it around to smack fish with a killing blow.

CORNERED: Whitetip reef sharks search for prey in crevices in a reef. Then they reach in with their narrow snouts to gobble up the prey.

CUTTING ATTACK: Saw sharks are named for their narrow snouts, which have sharp teeth sticking out on each side. The sharks use their sawlike snouts to slash and slice fish.

Saw sharks are BORN WITH THEIR TEETH FOLDED BACK against their snouts, probably to protect their mother from injury.

CRUSHING BITE: A tiger shark can chew through turtle shells. It has strong teeth that are jagged like a bread knife.

Tiger sharks get their name from the TIGERLIKE STRIPES they have when they're young.

CHAPTER 3

Shark Hall of Fame

The WORLD'S BIGGEST FISH is the WHALE SHARK.

The second-largest fish, the BASKING SHARK, can be 33 feet long—that's nearly the LENGTH OF A TELEPHONE POLE!

28

Whale sharks are gentle giants. They can be as long as a city bus and weigh as much as three African elephants. But they feed on some of the smallest living things in the sea: plankton. Whale sharks use their huge mouths to suck up these tiny plants and animals as they swim.

Let's meet some other record-setting members of the shark hall of fame!

The **SMALLEST KNOWN SHARK** is the dwarf lantern shark. It measures about **SEVEN INCHES LONG.**

Experts think that a great white shark's bite is
THREE TIMES STRONGER THAN A LION'S.

The great white shark lives up to its name. It weighs more than a hippopotamus, and it can be up to 20 feet long. This huge size makes the great white powerful enough to take on large prey such as sea lions and elephant seals.

great white shark

It also has more than 300 teeth! The first three rows of teeth are exposed, and several more rows are growing below the shark's gums. It uses the exposed teeth to rip its prey into pieces.

The extinct shark MEGALODON had the strongest bite in history: up to 10 TIMES MORE POWERFUL than a great white's.

Of all shark species, the COOKIECUTTER SHARK has the LARGEST TEETH for its body size.

The shortfin mako is the world's fastest shark, and one of the fastest fish on the planet. It zooms through the open ocean. There, it's on the hunt for prey such as fish, squid, rays, and even other sharks. Shortfin makos are so fast, they can leap right out of the water. They can reach heights of 15 feet!

shortfin mako shark

The goblin shark can THRUST ITS JAW FORWARD to snap up prey faster than any other shark.

The **SLOWEST SHARK** on Earth is the Greenland shark. It moves at less than **ONE MILE AN HOUR!**

The DEEPEST-LIVING SHARK is the Portuguese dogfish, commonly found nearly 10,000 FEET BELOW THE SURFACE.

Strangest Sharks

Meet some of the most unusual sharks in the sea.

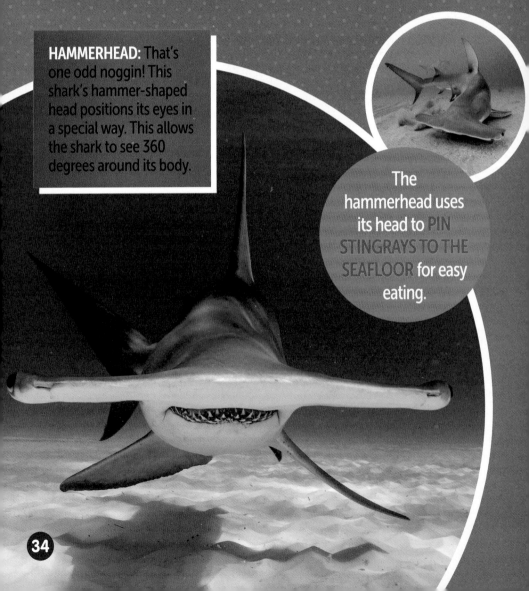

HAMMERHEAD: That's one odd noggin! This shark's hammer-shaped head positions its eyes in a special way. This allows the shark to see 360 degrees around its body.

The hammerhead uses its head to PIN STINGRAYS TO THE SEAFLOOR for easy eating.

FRILLED SHARK: The jaws of this creepy-looking creature are filled with three-pronged teeth.

The frilled shark is named for its GILLS, which have FRILLY EDGES.

MEGAMOUTH SHARK: Its name is no joke. The 16-foot megamouth shark has a mouth that's about four feet wide.

Prehistoric Sharks

Step back into prehistoric times and you'll find even odder sharks.

One ancient shark had a SPINE STICKING OUT of the back of its head.

SCISSOR-TOOTHED SHARK: This shark had a straight row of teeth on the top and bottom of its mouth. It may have used them like a pair of scissors to slice prey in half.

ANVIL SHARK: It looked much like a modern shark ... except for one thing. Its dorsal fin was the shape of an anvil! The fin's purpose is still a mystery.

Scientists think that the EARLIEST SHARKS may have been TOOTHLESS.

BUZZSAW SHARK: This shark had a spiral of teeth that filled its lower jaw. As it closed its mouth, the spiral would rotate backward—just like the circular blade of a buzz saw.

CHAPTER 4

Share the Seas

You are more likely to be CRUSHED BY A VENDING MACHINE than to be killed by a shark.

blacktip reef shark

Caribbean reef shark

Sharks are some of the most misunderstood creatures on the planet. With their big jaws and sharp teeth, they might seem scary. But in fact, sharks almost never bite people.

Sharks evolved millions of years before humans appeared on Earth. This means people aren't part of their diet. Sharks would much rather eat their natural prey, such as crabs, fish, squid, and seals.

39

Every year, humans kill about 100 MILLION SHARKS.

whale sharks

Fisheries often catch and kill sharks BY ACCIDENT WHEN FISHING for other species.

Humans are a much bigger danger to sharks than sharks are to humans. Sharks are hunted mainly for their fins, which are used to make a dish called shark fin soup in some countries.

Pollution also puts sharks in danger. Many sharks get caught in old fishing gear or accidentally swallow plastic trash that ended up in the ocean.

This tiger shark is tangled in a loop of rope.

Blacktip reef sharks swim among plastic trash.

ITEMS FOUND in one tiger shark's STOMACH included license plates, a fur coat, and a video camera.

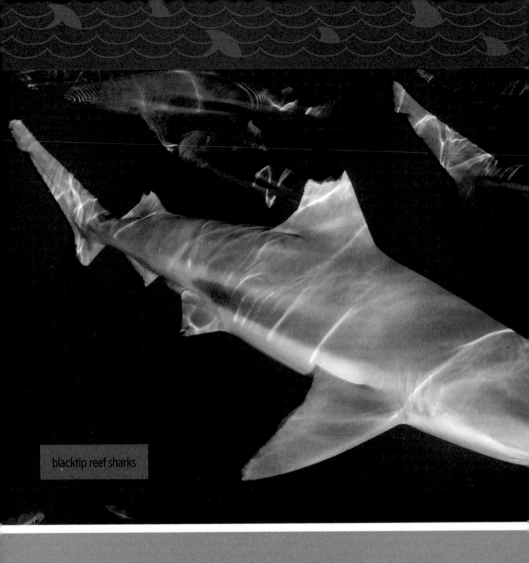

blacktip reef sharks

Today, more than 20 countries have banned hunting sharks for their fins. But people still hunt sharks illegally. It's important to protect sharks because they are one of the sea's major predators. They keep their prey animals' numbers at healthy levels. And this helps to keep the food chain in balance.

hammerhead shark

Sharks have used their sharp senses and hunting skills to thrive in Earth's oceans for a very long time. Keeping sharks healthy is key to keeping our oceans healthy, too.

1

The bonnethead shark is the only shark known to eat seagrass as part of its natural diet.

2

Most fish use an air-filled bladder to stay afloat, but sharks use an oil-filled liver.

3

Sharks have no vocal cords, and so they make no vocal sounds.

4

Sharks can travel long distances without stopping to eat by surviving on oil from their livers.

5

Some species of shark can turn their stomachs inside out through their mouths to get rid of shells, bones, and scales.

6

Baby sharks can shed teeth even before they're born.

7

Some sharks roll their eyes back into their heads to protect them when going after prey.

8

Lemon sharks return to their birthplace to have their young.

9

Bull sharks can live in both salt and freshwater.

10

Some sharks can go months without eating.

11

The megamouth shark wasn't discovered until 1976.

12 There are more than 500 species of sharks.

25 MORE FACTS

ABOUT SHARKS

13
Hammerheads' wide heads may give them a stronger sense of electroreception.

14
The cookiecutter shark is named for the round shape of the bites it takes out of its prey.

15
Whitetip reef sharks crowd into caves to rest, piling on top of one another.

16
Greenland sharks often have glowing parasites that attach to their eyes.

17
A shark's liver is enormous, making up as much as one-quarter of its body weight.

18
Great white sharks have blue-tinted eyes.

19
The horned shark's teeth are often stained purple from eating sea urchins.

20
Humans move just the lower jaw to bite, but sharks can move both their upper and lower jaws.

21
Some sharks have special heating organs that warm their eyes, helping them see better in colder water.

22
A young whale shark can eat 46 pounds of plankton a day.

23
A whale shark's skin is about four inches thick, making it the thickest skin of any animal.

24
Baby frilled sharks may grow inside their mother for as long as three and a half years before they are born.

25
Each whale shark has a pattern of spots as unique as a human fingerprint.

Shark Facts Roundup

1. Lantern sharks glow in the dark. 2. In 2005, scientists tracked a great white shark as it traveled 12,400 miles from Africa to Australia. 3. Adult female sharks are almost always bigger than adult male sharks. 4. Almost everything scientists know about shark evolution comes from shark teeth—usually the only thing left behind by prehistoric sharks. 5. The prehistoric megalodon was the largest shark that ever lived. It was 60 feet long—that's almost as long as a bowling lane! 6. Shark skin feels rough, like sandpaper. 7. It may not look like it, but sharks have ears—they're just inside their heads. 8. Sharks can only swim forward. 9. A great white shark can eat up to 11 tons of food in a year. That's about 11 times more than the average human eats! 10. Great white sharks are named for their white bellies. 11. Some sharks will enter a trancelike state when they are flipped onto their backs. 12. A few shark species live in freshwater rivers in India, Southeast Asia, and parts of Australia. 13. The goblin shark looks almost the same as it did 125 million years ago, when dinosaurs roamed Earth. 14. To figure out how old a shark is, scientists can look at a piece of its spine and count the bands like the rings of a tree. 15. Like cats, sharks have a reflective layer in their eyes that allows them to see well in the dark. 16. Basking sharks have been spotted traveling together in schools of 100. 17. Shortfin mako sharks can be 12 feet long and weigh 1,200 pounds. 18. Scientists believe that the Greenland shark may live for more than 400 years. 19. Walking sharks use their fins to "walk" along the seafloor—and sometimes even onto land! 20. The angel shark can attack and kill its prey in one-tenth of a second. 21. For most sharks, one-third of their brain is dedicated to their sense of smell. 22. Scientists think sharks may not see in color. 23. Great white sharks are the world's largest predatory fish, or fish that hunt. 24. Sixgill sharks can have more than 100 babies at a time. 25. A baby shark can sense a predator from inside its egg. 26. Sharks have large brains for their body size and are capable of learning. 27. Sharks don't chew their food. They rip off chunks and swallow them whole! 28. Sharks live in nearly all ocean habitats, from tropical reefs to chilly Arctic waters. 29. Sharks are fish. 30. Ancient sharks once shared the seas with giant swimming reptiles called mosasaurs and plesiosaurs. 31. Sharks have been on Earth since before the time of the dinosaurs. 32. Scientists have found fossils of more than 3,000 species of prehistoric sharks. 33. Once they reach their adult size, sharks keep growing slowly for the rest of their lives. 34. Sharks belong to a group of animals called elasmobranchs, which also includes rays and skates. 35. A great white shark can grow 50,000 teeth in its lifetime. 36. Some sharks replace their teeth every two weeks. 37. The outer coating of shark teeth is made of fluoride, the active ingredient in toothpaste. 38. Baby sharks are called pups. 39. Baby sharks swallow their own teeth before they're born, perhaps for the calcium. 40. Before it's born, a sand tiger shark pup feeds on its unborn siblings. 41. A shark's skin can shred a diver's wet suit. 42. Denticles are about as hard

as granite and can act like armor. 43 By mimicking shark skin, designers are working to create faster airplanes, cars, and drones. 44 There are at least 57 species of sharks that can glow. 45 The swell shark scares off predators by gulping water and swelling to twice its normal size. 46 The pocket shark can squirt a glowing liquid, probably to distract predators. 47 Great white sharks can detect as little as one drop of blood in 25 gallons of water. 48 Sharks have taste buds lining their mouths and throats, and will spit out a meal they don't like. 49 Some sharks have sensitive whiskers around their mouths that they use to taste the ocean floor, searching for buried prey. 50 Great white sharks use electroreception to sense a fish's breathing. 51 Using electroreception to sense Earth's magnetic field, sharks can swim in a perfectly straight line for miles. 52 Researchers use decoy seals to study great white sharks' hunting habits. 53 The wobbegong's huge head is wider than it is long. 54 Saw sharks are born with their teeth folded back against their snouts, probably to protect their mother from injury. 55 Tiger sharks get their name from the tigerlike stripes they have when they're young. 56 The world's biggest fish is the whale shark. 57 The second-largest fish, the basking shark, can be 33 feet long—that's nearly the length of a telephone pole! 58 The smallest known shark is the dwarf lantern shark. It measures about seven inches long. 59 Experts think that a great white shark's bite is three times stronger than a lion's. 60 The extinct shark megalodon had the strongest bite in history: up to 10 times more powerful than a great white's. 61 Of all shark species, the cookiecutter shark has the largest teeth for its body size. 62 The shortfin mako can reach a top speed of 50 miles an hour—faster than a racehorse! 63 The goblin shark can thrust its jaw forward to snap up prey faster than any other shark. 64 The slowest shark on Earth is the Greenland shark. It moves at less than one mile an hour! 65 The deepest-living shark is the Portuguese dogfish, commonly found nearly 10,000 feet below the surface. 66 The hammerhead uses its head to pin stingrays to the seafloor for easy eating. 67 The frilled shark is named for its gills, which have frilly edges. 68 One ancient shark had a spine sticking out of the back of its head. 69 Scientists think that the earliest sharks may have been toothless. 70 You are more likely to be crushed by a vending machine than to be killed by a shark. 71 Most sharks need to eat only every two to three days. 72 Every year, humans kill about 100 million sharks. 73 Fisheries often catch and kill sharks by accident when fishing for other species. 74 Around half of shark species are threatened by extinction. 75 Items found in one tiger shark's stomach included license plates, a fur coat, and a video camera. 76 The bonnethead shark is the only shark known to eat seagrass as part of its natural diet. 77 Most fish use an air-filled bladder to stay afloat, but sharks use an oil-filled liver. 78 Sharks have no vocal cords, and so they make no vocal sounds. 79 Sharks can travel long distances without stopping to eat by surviving on oil from their livers. 80 Some species of shark can turn their stomachs inside out through their mouths to get rid of shells, bones, and scales. 81 Baby sharks can shed teeth even before they're born. 82 Some sharks roll their eyes back into their heads to protect them when going after prey. 83 Lemon sharks return to their birthplace to have their young. 84 Bull sharks can live in both salt and freshwater. 85 Some sharks can go months without eating. 86 The megamouth shark wasn't discovered until 1976. 87 There are more than 500 species of sharks. 88 Hammerheads' wide heads may give them a stronger sense of electroreception. 89 The cookiecutter shark is named for the round shape of the bites it takes out of its prey. 90 Whitetip reef sharks crowd into caves to rest, piling on top of one another. 91 Greenland sharks often have glowing parasites that attach to their eyes. 92 A shark's liver is enormous, making up as much as one-quarter of its body weight. 93 Great white sharks have blue-tinted eyes. 94 The horned shark's teeth are often stained purple from eating sea urchins. 95 Humans move just the lower jaw to bite, but sharks can move both their upper and lower jaws. 96 Some sharks have special heating organs that warm their eyes, helping them see better in colder water. 97 A young whale shark can eat 46 pounds of plankton a day. 98 A whale shark's skin is about four inches thick, making it the thickest skin of any animal. 99 Baby frilled sharks may grow inside their mother for as long as three and a half years before they are born. 100 Each whale shark has a pattern of spots as unique as a human fingerprint.

INDEX

Boldface indicates illustrations.